THE RESTAURANT COACH™ PLAYBOOK

365 INSIDE TIPS TO KEEP YOU AT THE TOP OF YOUR GAME

DONALD BURNS
THE RESTAURANT COACH™

The Restaurant Coach Playbook

365 Inside Tips To Keep You
At The Top Of Your Game

DONALD BURNS
THE RESTAURANT COACH™

Copyright © 2023 by Donald Burns

Donald Burns, The Restaurant Coach™

donald@therestaurantcoach.com

www.therestaurantcoach.com

All rights reserved. No part of this book may be reproduced or transmitted in any form or by any means without written permission from the author.

This book is designed to provide accurate and authoritative information about the subject matter covered. This information is given with the understanding that the author is not engaged in rendering legal, professional advice. Since the details of your situation are fact dependent, you should always seek the services of a competent professional.

DISCLAIMER

The author provides the book in its entirety, including its content, services, and data (collectively, "Information") contained therein, and only for the purposes of information. No professional, financial, lifestyle or medical advice is provided in this book, and the information should not be used or understood to be professional advice.

EXPLICIT LANGUAGE

Author's Note: If you are sensitive to language, then you might want to stop here. The material in this booklet is written in real world terms and language that occurs in restaurants.

Please note that I don't use profanity to offend anyone. I use language to break your thinking patterns and make you uncomfortable. When you get to that place, then (and only then) will you start taking action to change.

That being said, I have worked in restaurants and kitchens for over nearly four decades and yes, I do drop the F-Bomb quite often. Let's have a fucking great time getting you the restaurant and life you know deep down that you want. See, I warned you...

DEDICATION

To those that will not settle for meciocrity.

> **"THE TROUBLE IS YOU THINK YOU HAVE TIME."**
>
> –Jack Kornfield

HOW IT STARTED

Over the years, I have posted quite a few of The Restaurant Coach™ Tips across the Internet. Some of my clients asked if there was a booklet available where they could see them all. I never thought about it, but it was a great idea. Here are —365 of my tips that you can use to trigger critical concepts and keep your edge.

Working with some of the best and most talented people in the industry (including Wolfgang Puck), I have found that getting to the top of the industry is not that hard. Not to say it's easy; it just requires an action plan and taking massive consistent action daily. The real struggle comes when you get to the top and then relax because you feel you made it. Working for Wolfgang was like getting a Ph.D. in branding success. For the last 40 years, he has not only been at the top of the restaurant game, and he continues to stay there and expand his brand year after year!

Here is my playbook of motivational saying and sometimes just a straight kick in the ass.

If you don't know my story, I grew up in kitchens (my father was a Gordon Ramsey-type executive chef who ruled his kitchen with an iron fist and razor-sharp swords. He knew just what to say to make you crumble. I've seen grown men break down and cry in the kitchen from the word my dad would shout to them. His only reply when someone had broken down was, "Go cry in the walk-in."

One day he was yelling at a cook in his office. "What culinary school did you go to!" He demanded.

The (now shaking cook) replied, "The CIA (Culinary Institute Of America) Chef."

My dad, "You know what I want you to do? Call them."

The line cook looked very confused, "Call them?"

"Yes, now.", my father replied.

"What should I say." The cook inquired.

Then my dad lost it and exploded, "I want you to ask them for your money back because you haven't learned a damn thing!"

The entire kitchen (including myself) would freeze up, and there would be a weird silence to the kitchen. It was like being the prey of a T-Rex; if we didn't move, maybe he wouldn't see us.

My father was a brilliant chef. **As a leader, he ruled by fear.**

When I became a young chef, that was my only model of what a "chef" acted like as a leader, so I followed suit. I look back now and am not surprised by the high turnover I had during my early career. **Ego and anger are a deadly combination.**

My first real "chef" job was at a tiny restaurant in New Mexico called The Lost Oasis Café. Okay, small might even be an exaggeration...it was only ten tables. I was 24 at the time and was hired as the Sous Chef. The chef was a pretty big name out of Albuquerque. I was at first curious why a "big named" chef from Albuquerque would come to a small tome to run a very small café. I soon found my answer as the chef would disappear for hours to his little apartment above the café and return smelling of alcohol. About four weeks into the new restaurant opening, he got into a big screaming match with the owner about the size of French fry and walked out. I was promoted to chef.

Many chef promotions are this kind of battlefield promotion. The chef gets fired or walks out and the Sous Chef is automatically promoted. Sometimes this is a bad idea, especially if the Sous Chef has very little management or leadership training. In my case, I had a bad model of how a chef should act. Not knowing any better than, I went with what I knew.

I was the typical asshole chef back then. I demanded the food be eaten the way I envisioned. What? They want the Demi Glacé on the side? No fucking way! This is my food! My menu! They will eat it my way!

One day the owner (Scott) pulled me into the office for a talk. I have to admit I was nervous because the last time he brought the chef into the office, it didn't turn out so well for the chef!

Scott was a very kind and soft-spoken man. He sat down behind the desk and the conversation went like this:

Scott: "You know I really love your food and so do the guests. We have been written up a few times by well-known travel writers and it's been great for business."

Me: "Thanks Scott."

Scott: "One thing I need to talk to you about is..."

Here it comes I thought.

Scott: "You know how you won't make substitutions or allow guests to get the sauce on the side?"

Me: "Yeah..."

Scott: "Well, if those guests are not happy, they won't be back and if they don't come back, I won't be able to pay you anymore."

Me thinking...

Me: "So, it's not about me, it's about the guest?"

Scott: "Now, you get it."

After that conversation, I made a 180-degree attitude change about substitutions and it lead me to question, how I ruled the kitchen with an iron fist. I realized that I hated the way my father ran the kitchen with fear and yelling, and yet, here I was being a mini version of him. That wasn't me. I learned more like how my martial arts instructor taught me...with explaining the why and patience. Like a coach.

Over the next year I read more about leadership and changed my approach to how I was as a chef and surprisingly, people started to hear that I was a good chef to learn from and started to ask if I had any opening in the kitchen. I've never looked back.

HOW TO USE THIS PLAYBOOK

Over the coming pages you will find 365 of my very best tips, quotes, and gold nuggets that I use when working with my clients. Many have become a signature for me and The Restaurant Coach™ brand. If you have ever heard me speak either on stage or watched one of my videos on my YouTube channel, you might recognize a few of them.

I do this on purpose because I find that repetition is the key to learning. I will say these over and over until my clients starts saying them to me without a prompt! Then I know they have rewired their brain with a new mindset and belief.

Your beliefs are the foundation of reaching success whether you know it or not. It's called **The Success Cycle** and for long term results you have to master it!

The best way to use these is take one each day and see how you can apply it to your restaurant and your life. Some might seem very apparent, and others will require you to think about it. Remember that the truth will set you free, but first it will piss you off.

Take these quotes and share them with your team and even on social media. Tag me and you might just win a ticket to my annual Restaurant Success Summit in Arizonia where my elite coaching groups Restaurant Masterminds and The Restaurant Accelerator get together for 3-day to listen to 6 industry experts show them how to set their restaurant up for massive success. Use #therestaurantcoach #donaldburns #TRCplaybook and I might just see you at the summit!

THE SUCCESS CYCLE

Remember Newton's first law of motion? An object in motion stays in motion; an object at rest stays at rest. The same s true with your restaurant. If you're moving and gaining ground, you're likely to keep reaping rewards. But if you're stuck, well, getting going takes some serious effort.

THE FOUR MINUTE MILE

Pre-1954, experts asserted that the human body was simply not capable of running a mile in under four minutes. Not only was it apparently dangerous, but it was also impossible.

However, on 6th May 1954, Roger Bannister broke the four-minute barrier, recording a time of 3:59.4 to become the first man to run a sub four-minute mile. Just 46 days later, John Landy broke the record again with a time of 3:57.9, becoming the second man to break the four-minute mile barrier. Within two years, 37 more men managed the same feat, and thousands have since done the same. In fact, running a mile in under four minutes is the standard for all professional middle distance runners.

So, what was it that lead to such a domino effect? What allowed Roger Bannister to break the four-minute mile was belief? The answer is the belief that he could.

Not only did Bannister break the time barrier, but he broke the psychological barrier the idea that, as the so-called experts had claimed running a mile in less than four minutes was impossible.

When Bannister's competitors realized that it was possible, this raised their own belief which in turn allowed them to tap deeper into their potential. The mere fact that they knew it was possible produced within them a sense of certainty which motivated them to train harder and focus on achieving the feat themselves. This is a classic example of the Success Cycle.

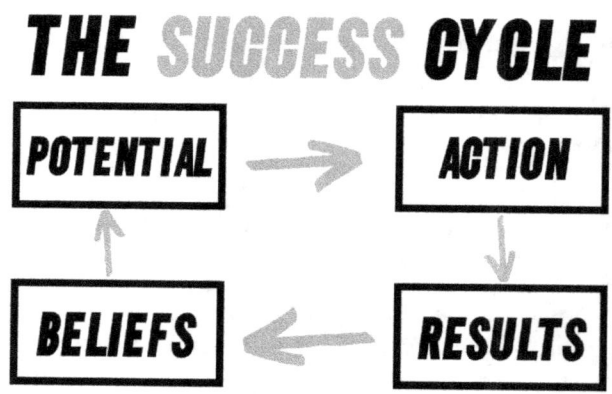

There are four distinct stages to the Success Cycle: Belief, Potential, Action and Results.

Our beliefs determine our potential, our potential determines out actions and our actions determine our results. The more belief we have, the more potential we tap into, the better actions we take and ultimately the better results we get.

Let's unpack each of these four stages in more detail.

BELIEF

Belief refers to the sense of certainty we have about what we can achieve.

We get what we expect. If we expect failure, we increase the likelihood that we will get failure. If we expect success, we increase the likelihood that we will get success.

When we don't believe maximize our belief, we tend to exert less effort. Therefore, our level of certainty determines how much potential we can tap into.

POTENTIAL

Human beings are extraordinary. We all have unlimited potential. We are all capable of success. Unfortunately however, most people only tap into a tiny amount of their true potential.

When we don't maximize our potential, we instantly limit what we are capable of. Therefore, how much potential we tap into determines the actions we take.

ACTION

When we tap into more of our potential, it follows that we will take more effective action. In contrast, when we tap into only a small amount of our potential, naturally we will take a small amount of action.

When we don't maximize our action, we limit the types of results we can get. Therefore, how much action we take determines the results we get.

RESULTS

Our results simply reflect our original beliefs.

When we fail, it reaffirms our original belief that we were going to fail and so we are likely to have less belief the next time we do it. When we succeed, it reaffirms our original belief that we were going to succeed, which in turns gives us more belief and confidence the next time we do it.

Therefore, the results we get determines how much belief we have in ourselves, thus forming a cycle.

"SUCCESS BREEDS CONFIDENCE BREEDS SUCCESS."

Restaurant success is all about momentum and understanding the success cycle can be key to getting the results you want. The cycle of success shows that what you do impacts your results, which then impact the choices you make, impacting your results. In other words: What you put in; you take out. This applies to life in general and can more specifically be tied into the business success your company experiences.

Now what goes up doesn't need to go down.

The laws of physics don't always apply to restaurant success. That's because we have factors like your beliefs and attitudes. In many ways your belief, attitude and certainty is the fuel that powers your success cycle. The more success you have, the more you'll believe you're going to succeed. If you've experienced success, you're more likely to exude confidence and take risks, which can lead to greater rewards. Then the cycle begins again since you gain more certainty from your positive results.

WARNING: Sometimes when you are on a downward spiral you keep going down.

Why? You're in a negative feedback loop. Therefore, many feel like they're trapped and can never reach real business success. It doesn't have to be huge problems, either – even tiny details can keep a downward spiral in motion. After experiencing enough setbacks, we start to stack those problems until they seem insurmountable.

Here's an example: You reach out to hire a new GM and you find a person that stays just a few weeks and quits. Then you hire another and after a month they leave. Your negative belief kicks in and you start to think that "there are no good people out there".

With diminished potential, your interviews become shorter and less detailed (Less action), leading to more poor results. Clearly, one of the key factors for restaurant success is learning to reverse a downward trajectory.

Stuck in the negative and want to break the cycle? You can put yourself in a more positive place and achieve restaurant success. Here's how to start a cycle of success, no matter what you're doing. Remember, the keys to success in business aren't just groundless positive thinking or sending out requests to the universe; it's setting yourself up to take the actions you need to get the results you want. Think of it as reprogramming the cycle to achieve what you really want.

Remember, your mindset, your state is all you need to fuel an ongoing upward trajectory. The concept of state ties in directly to the concept of momentum in the success cycle. You can change your perspective and feelings through physical movement and awareness-building. Your basic body mechanics, breathing patterns, thoughts and feelings all impact each other, which is a valuable tool in learning to manage your emotions. By learning to tweak one feeling, you learn to tweak them all.

As a restaurant owner, using mind-body techniques to achieve a state of calm, clarity and direction prepares you to manage your business decisions so that you catalyze forward movement.

That's why these daily quotes are so powerful *(if you use them)*.

Remember: resourcefulness is the ultimate resource. Understand how to cultivate a mindset of finding a way instead of giving up; your restaurant will thank you.

*IF ALL THE WORLD IS A STAGE.
I SUGGEST YOU START
PERFORMING AT YOUR BEST.*

THE RESTAURANT COACH™
DAILY TIPS

1. If your restaurant sucks it's because you suck running it. No one said you had to be perfect. Sometimes you're not the right person for the job. Admit when things are not 100% the way you want it and just be honest that t sucks a little. Now take action to change it.

2. All business problems are really people problems in disguise. *Here is the other side of that: all people problems are communication problems.*

3. The people who think they are irreplaceable, are usually the one that are very easy to replace. Just remember that while people themselves are irreplaceable, job positions can be easily changed.

4. Please fix typos on your menu. They send a message that you just don't care. Plus, it just makes you look like an amateur.

5. Profit is not a dirty word. Even those there are plenty of people that will try to tell you it is!

6. A lot of restaurant owners operate from the zone of denial and delusion. Mediocre restaurants are a disease; coaching is the cure. If you feel like your restaurant is running you, then call me.

7. If you don't know your numbers, you don't know your business. In fact, you don't have a business. What you really have is a hobby, a very expensive hobby!

8. Great restaurants don't hire skilled people and motivate them, they hire motivated people and train them consistently and constantly. Training is what separates the good, from the great, from the outstanding!

9. Culture flows down not up, culture starts with you. How is the flow of culture in your restaurant?

10. Hope is not a strategy for running a restaurant. Well, not one that you want to invest in.

11. Anyone with money can open a restaurant. Staying open and making a steady profit is the real challenge.

12. C players cost you three times the cost of hiring an A player. You get what you pay for.

13. A pre-shift meeting sets the tone for service. No pre-shift at your restaurant? Then you get what you deserve.... unfocused service.

14. Mediocrity will suffocate your restaurant. Never let it in your door. Once you do it is like a vampire that will drain your culture and will cripple your business.

15. Every time you hire someone you are adding to your marketing team. Be extremely careful about who you let on your team.

16. Don't tell me you have to do everything yourself because you don't trust your team. That is bullshit! If you do not trust your people to do their jobs, then find people you do! A true leader does not stand in the way of the team. I have a saying that if you cannot spot the negative person in your restaurant bringing everyone down....it's you.

17. Restaurants get better when the people in them become better people. That of course starts with you!

18. You must know that your people are much more than an expense line. It's funny how owners say that their people are their most valuable asset and yet they don't treat them like that.

19. Nothing is as powerful as saying THANK YOU. The best thing is that it's free so throw them around liberally.

20. Ego, pride, control issues and denial have closed more restaurants than you can imagine. It's sad because many could have been saved.

21. Most managers do not understand resource allocation. If you do not pay your top talent what they are worth, they will find a company that will.

22. A lot of restaurant owners operate from the zone of denial and delusion. Mediocre restaurants are a disease, coaching is the cure.

23. Expect more from yourself than you do from others. You will never have the restaurant you want if you cannot hold yourself to a higher standard then you hold your team! Don't be that manager who is upset when staff shows up late, yet they routinely stroll in 30-40 minutes late themselves. Don't be that chef who is upset when their team does not show them respect, yet they call people names and talk down to the team. Culture is created by the core values you exemplify. What kind of role model are you being for your restaurant?

24. Be objective about your menu. Read it like a guests would. Does it make sense? Are there words people might not know? Getting a fresh view about your menu can open up opportunities for growth of your brand. That always means dropping the ego.

25. Good has become the standard because we have accepted mediocrity. Stop settling for good because it really sucks to be average.

26. We use the word team so much that it has become diluted. I would go as far as challenging you that the people who work with you at your restaurant are not a true team. They are a group. How can you tell the difference? One simple attitude shift: groups are selfish while a true team is selfless.

27. The old saying that "people are your most important asset" is wrong. The RIGHT people are your most important asset! Do yourself and them a favor.... don't keep bad employees.

28. You don't control time, your control your attention. Q: What is distraction really costing you each day?

29. Those that are the most productive schedule "focus blocks" each day to make sure they are working on tasks that move their life and business forward.

30. Social Media is about being social. Don't just talk about what your special is for today. There are hundreds of other restaurants in your market doing just that. Stand out and get creative. Say you are a pizza chain...how about holding an online photo contest that lets people post unusual places eating pizza out of your pizza box? Rules are simple: You need to see the logo and most likes, retweets or hearts on Twitter, Facebook or Instagram gets a prize.

31. Who you hire is more important than you think. It can be stressful running short staffed, however letting the wrong people on your team can damage customer service and pull apart your current team. Always hire for character over skills. Skills you can teach and train. Character you cannot.

32. Do want you say you are going to do. Nothing destroys your credibility faster than not following through with what you said. Your staff doesn't like it and your customers won't come back because of it. Teach and train this throughout your restaurant because everyone must be on the same page. Example: the server takes an order for a medium rare hamburger and the cooks ignore it and send out a well-done burger. You just lost face from the customer's point of view.

33. Place your mission and core values where customers can see it! As an owner or operator, one of your goals is to tell people what you believe in!

34. Number one reason people leave their job is lack of acknowledgment and appreciation. Have you communicated with your team today that you appreciate them?

35. If you want a life beyond your restaurant, then you have to build a strong team! One person shows don't last very long in the restaurant industry.

36. As soon as we introduce change, old habits will dig in and fight with those new one for fear of being replaced. Many times, we take the easy path instead of the right path. It is a sad reflection that we have lost our passion. You are a brand. What are your core values? What does your brand stand for? Be that.

37. Restaurant culture is like a sourdough starter...you must feed it every day, or it will die.

38. Many managers are so concerned about losing their jobs that they forgot to really DO their job. You were hired to protect the owner's interest in their investment by producing an exception guest experience, managing the numbers, and building the brand.

39. 81% of professionals say "yes" to change, however only 10% will take action to support that. Talk without doing something is just that... "talk". Do it and do it now!

40. You must have faith in yourself, before you can have faith in others.

41. When would NOW be a good time?

42. Employee retention has a bigger impact on sales then most restaurant owners realize. Manage your turnover by making it a highly selective process to make it on your team. Create a culture of excellence no matter what kind of concept you have. You can be world class if you are a taco food truck or a five-star restaurant. Excellence is a state of mind!

43. Are you promoting the right people? Sometimes we promote due to tenure. But is that putting the right person in the right job playing to their strengths? Behavioral surveys can help you make better team placements within your restaurant.

44. You must have the food right. It has to be perfect; it has to be consistent, and it has to have a 'wow effect.' You also have to have the right people in the right position. Unfortunately, in many restaurants it's the managers who are not the right person for the position.

45. Everyone's behavior makes sense to themselves in the moment. Even if it doesn't make sense to you!

46. Beware of hidden agendas. Sometimes people will buy in and even agree to the plan, then their actions don't seem to be going in the direction they agreed upon. That's a hidden and personal agenda. Those little secret agendas destroy relationships.

47. Advice from my father: When you find yourself in a hole...stop digging.

48. Your restaurant is exactly the way you want it to be. If you wanted it to be different or better, you would have taken action to change it.

49. You want to grow your restaurant brand in control. Always in control, never out of control. Growing when you are not ready is like playing chess and trying to capture the other player's king in just one move.

50. There is the culture you think you have and the culture you really have. My experience is that most restaurants don't have the culture they think they have.

51. If leadership is lacking in your restaurant, you need to look just at yourself. Self-leadership begets team leadership.

52. Real control does not come from controlling others, it comes from controlling yourself...your emotions and mindset.

53. Entitlement is one of the warning signs of a toxic culture.

54. If you don't take an active role in the creation of your restaurant culture you're likely to get one that you don't want.

55. Negativity breeds complacency. Complacency invites mediocrity. Mediocrity is death to your restaurant. **It's a natural law of restaurants.**

56. Great cultures endure. Great cultures become iconic. Great cultures are built. Great cultures start with you.

57. When you honor your core values, you honor your true self. When you live by a clear set of values, it is easier to align your life with your goals. When you are living your core values with authenticity and integrity you are a leader people will want to work for and follow.

58. Behavior does predict performance.

59. Talk to your team about your expectations. Don't assume they get it. If you can't measure it, you can't manage it.

60. The cure for procrastination is to take action! *Like, immediate action!*

61. If it's constantly crazy at your restaurant, then I have two words for you: fuck that. I have another two as well: stop it.

62. The biggest battle you will face is between what you know and what you feel.

63. Your life purpose starts where you are right now. You can't wait for things to be perfect because they never will be. The first step to getting the life you desire is to act in the face of things not being ideal.

64. We all have fears. It's how we handle those fears that separates us.

65. When you're great you trust your instincts. When you're outstanding, your instincts trust you.

66. Success doesn't happen by projecting expectations outward. It happens by cultivating presence inward. Be in the moment. Act now.

67. The most dangerous move is to play it safe. Mediocrity loves to disguise itself as the safe move.

68. Your mindset drives and shapes everything you do weather you realize it or not. Do you behave calmly in adversity or if you blow up over something others deem just not that important? The human mind does (and will) play tricks on you. Don't think that your mindset is any different. It's wired to survive... your survival. Sometimes it doesn't make the rational decision, it makes the call that is going to keep you around. Self-preservation is a human instinct.

69. Most restaurants are doing the best they can. Most also don't realized that good enough isn't good at all. Good is average. **Being average sucks!**

70. You can say this and that. You can try to put on a mask and pretend to be someone else. It's your core values that are constantly reflected in your actions and behavior that tell who you truly are.

71. If you have ever said to one of your staff, "Do it because I'm your boss." You are not the boss, you're just a bully. True leadership commands behavior by the example they set. Managers and bosses demand behavior because they have no credibility with their team!

72. If your entertainment budget exceeds your education budget, that is why you are stuck in mediocrity and complacency. Your life will never rise about the level that you are at currently. Each new level of success requires a new version of you! New mindset, new habits, and new tools.

73. So many restaurant managers go to work with the goal not to lose their job. What they should be doing is remembering and doing their real job which is to become better leaders, grow the team, protect the brand, and amplify the guest experience.

74. If your restaurant isn't going exactly as your envisioned, then you need to ask better questions that challenge the status quo.... What is stepping on your cash flow? What is your strategy for this year? How are you attracting top talent? What is your development plan for your team leaders? What is your personal development plan? When things are not the way you want, I can tell you that you are focused on the wrong things. You've gotten comfortable and that is deadly in today's economy.

75. If you really want success, then you must back yourself into a corner. Give yourself no choice but to succeed. Let the consequences of failure become so horrific and so unthinkable that you'll have no choice but to do whatever it takes to get the restaurant and life you really want!

76. When you are fueled by fear, everything seems urgent, and the small stuff becomes huge. Relax, nothing is really under control.

77. Your restaurant is a silhouette of you. Every habit an outline. Every beat reflects your heart. Search inside yourself over these next few days and find that heartbeat of your restaurant within you.

78. Something to consider: You might have the right item on your menu in the wrong menu position.

79. You can't hang out with jackasses and expect to be a racehorse! You also can't build an epic brand with basic people! Time to level up your team.

80. Everyone has the ability to learn. Those that become outstanding constantly apply what they learn to become more.

81. There is a difference between training your team and taming your team. When you train your team, you harness and focus their natural strengths to higher levels. When you tame your team, you suppress those natural strengths and make them less.

82. Time is relentless and merciless! You need to treat time the same damn way. What are you doing today to become better?

83. There's a voice inside you that is full of doubt, hesitation, and will second guess your action. I have one too. We all do. It's fear. And it's job is to protect you. Fear just wants to be recognized and respected. You don't have to do what fear asks. Listen to it and softly tell that voice, "Listen, I know you are trying to protect me. I got this. So just shut the fuck up and watch me" Please don't misunderstand that danger is real. Fear is a choice.

84. The double edge sword of success is that it can leave you open to become lazy and complacent. There is always more you can do. More you can become.

85. Don't worry about the competition, make them worry about you! To do that you must aim to stand out in your market. Market domination is the answer.

86. If someone came in and observed your restaurant in action for 30 minutes, would they get a clear sense of what your culture was? How about what your standards are? Could they say what your brand is in one to two sentences? If not, you should think about why?

87. Consider for a moment how hard it is to just change yourself and you'll finally see what little chance you have of changing other people.

88. It's not knowing your strengths that gets you the restaurant you want, it's knowing your blind spots and learning how to manage them that does.

89. If you have a problem that can be solved by taking action, you don't have a problem.

90. People would rather explain their life than take action and actually do something to improve it. *Which is really sad.*

91. Mediocrity is a virus. And like all viruses it doesn't kill you right away. No. It settles in and slowly grows until in eventually consumes its host. After depleting you, taking your spirit, it leaves you a shell of who you once were.

92. Be grateful for those people in your life that lift you up and avoid those that try to pull you back down to their level of mediocrity.

93. One common issue many restaurants face...you can't see the problem if you are the problem.

94. No plan survives first contact with reality. Even the best-laid plans can go awry when they encounter unexpected obstacles or changes in the real world. Plans may need to be adjusted or altered as they are put into action. This is often referred to as "adaptability" or "agility" in planning and decision-making. Be flexible and adapt.

95. You can't solve a problem you're not willing to have. Addressing a challenge or issue requires a certain level of commitment and willingness to confront it head-on. If one is not open to acknowledging the existence of a problem or does not want to deal with it, it will be difficult or impossible to find a solution.

96. If your restaurant is not being copied, then you don't have your brand at the outstanding level.

97. During my days in Pararescue we were conditioned to think that "failure is not an option". In the restaurant industry failure is a **very real option** that you must deal with. If you are not innovating and risk losing something...then you're being complacent.

98. You either pay the price of mediocrity or invest in what it takes to become outstanding. ***Your choice.***

99. Growing your restaurant is about being responsible and accountable to the brand. Just because you can run fast (and open more locations) doesn't mean you don't need a solid strategy.

100. When you've become someone different (your future self) you no longer need motivation to keep it going because you go from what you "do" to what you "are". That is a beautiful place to be!

101. If you declare to the world that you are a "winner", you're not. You're a pretender. Winners don't announce it; **they just prove it.**

102. Working long hours in a restaurant is not a badge of honor, it's a mark of stupidity, piss poor planning, lack of priorities, failure to develop your team, and fear of saying no. The answer isn't more hours, it's less bullshit.

103. You can have the biggest most audacious goals in the world, however, if you don't develop the habits and mindset to become the person who can achieve those goals, they will just stay out there on the horizon...unattainable. Big goals require you to become a better person.

104. Leadership is often two-fold, one part is all about how you influence people, and the other is truly about how the world influences you. You need both to be a true leader.

105. We believe what we want to believe in. Once we take that in and feed those beliefs, they become self-filling prophecies. You believe there are no good people out in your market to hire, you won't find any. You believe your staff is a bunch of idiots that is all you'll see. If you believe you're a terrible leader, then you rise to the level of your own expectations. Thoughts turn into beliefs and beliefs turn into your life.

106. How dare you settle for average when the market has made it so easy to be outstanding! When you play below your potential you dishonor your strengths and your restaurant.

107. Where I am now is a result of who I was. Where I go, depends entirely on who I choose to be today. That's the best thing...you have a choice of who you choose to be.

108. We try to avoid pain, yet it is the one thing that lets us know what life truly is. Pain allows us to appreciate the good. Embrace the pain in your restaurant right now because it is your path to getting the restaurant you really want!

109. Bad management doesn't just happen; you allow it to happen. Now that you know that what are you going to do to change it?

110. If your standards are not considered a little unreasonable, then they are simply not high enough.

111. Stop texting or emailing your staff with problems or complaints about performance! That is a conversation to have face-to-face. Blowing up their phone or inbox with your rants, it just makes you look like the passive aggressive ass.

112. You can choose one of three options to any experience that happens to you: give in, get mad, or get creative and find a solution.

113. People say time changes things, but it's not true. Doing things changes things. Not doing things leaves things exactly as they were.

114. For all its ups and down. The hours. The joy and the frustrations. You love the restaurant business. There is nothing like seeing people having a great time in your restaurant. Smiling. Creating memories. Celebrating life. Let's work together to make this an industry we can be proud of. Break down the walls that divide us. No more front of the house versus back of the house. No day shift versus night shift. Be one team.. One mission. One house.

115. Look for what is missing. Many know how to improve what's there, but few can see what isn't there.

116. Here's the difference between a manager and a leader: A manager has employees that work FOR them. A leader works FOR their employees.

117. Always be moving forward. Never stop investing. Never stop improving. Never stop doing something new. The moment you stop improving your organization, it starts to die. Make it your goal to be better each and every day, in some small way. Remember the Japanese concept of Kaizen. Small daily improvements eventually result in huge advantages.

118. Anything that is not managed will deteriorate. If you want to uncover problems you don't know about, take a few moments, and look closely at the areas you haven't examined for a while. I guarantee you problems will be there.

119. Don't take yourself too seriously. Lighten up. Often, at least half of what we accomplish is due to luck. None of us are in control as much as we like to think we are.

120.

When it comes to getting results for your restaurant, I can say with 100% certainty (from working with over 400 restaurants a year) that 20% is systems and 80% is mindset! No bullshit. It's not that system, software, or process that you think of as a silver bullet to fix all the things that are wrong with your restaurant. Those are external tools. Your 80% is the mindset you and your team have. Like Dorothy in the Wizard of Oz, you have always had the power, you just never realized it! That's why those new checklists, new software, and new systems never get the results you want. You're focused on the wrong end of the equation. You're focused on the 20%. If you start working on the 80%, you will have a different restaurant and a different life...I promise.

121.

I don't fix restaurant problems; I fix the mindset that created the problem in the first place. Once you fix that the problems seem to fix themselves.

122.

Being comfortable is dangerous. When you are in your comfort zone, you are vulnerable. If you are not adapting to keep pace or better yet, stay innovative and ahead of the pack, you'll quickly find yourself displaced in your market. Your comfort zone is a place where bad habits hang out. They're like old friends, and no one wants to get rid of an old friend, especially if you've known them since childhood. Some of those habits have been living up in your head for a long time, rent-free. It's time to start writing some eviction notices.

123. You sometimes must do something you've never done to get something you've never had. You have been doing the same thing over and over for years (creating unconscious habits). Time to break free and pull away from your normal patterns. Time to learn some new things. The minute you stop learning, you start dying. To be successful, you need the right knowledge. Then you need to be relentless in applying that knowledge through the right actions. Consistently. Don't talk about it. **Fucking do something with it!**

124. The reason you may not be getting things done and moving your restaurant forward is that you are standing at the crossroads of should and must, thinking way too much. Hesitation and overthinking are chains holding you stuck. What's the cure? Stop thinking and start doing!

125. Restaurants are a living thing. They have good days and bad days. They grow. They mature. They undergo different phases of growth and change. **Every phase in your restaurant's life will require a different you.** You are the catalyst for change and culture. Restaurants get better when the people in them become better, and that starts with you becoming a better leader.

126. What you put up with, you end up with. Your restaurant and your life are a reflection of what you tolerate.

127. The ego can be self-sabotaging. Arrogance demands attention and allocates in the present. Most people don't think they need to improve. Arrogance blinds people to the world around them. Without awareness, people cannot see a need to change. Without leadership, a team cannot thrive. Without humility, all the talent in the world is useless.

128. Raise Your Standards First, Then Get Others to Raise Theirs If there's one thing that is sure to help you break free from the average, it's to raise your standards. It's easy to say you'll raise your standards and not do anything about it. Most people do this. It's called talking a good game. Your words and your actions must be congruent if you're going to be taken seriously as a leader. Hypocrisy is a team killer.

129. You are working hard to build your team, and maybe things don't seem right. The team does not gel together. You read the blog posts and books. You feel like you are doing and saying the right things…so what happened? The best intentions are nothing without the right execution. Knowing what to do is very different than doing what you know.

130. Communication issues account for most restaurant issues. It's either lack of communication or miscommunication. Mixed messages are a covert form of sabotage within your restaurant.

131. Look at the word manager. What is the first part of that word? Manage. A manager manages the day-to-day grind and never really gets ahead on tasks. These are the people who allow the restaurant to run them. They are always busy, but they are not very effective in building a team that can thrive. Managers are in survival mode. Now, look at the word leader. What is the first part of that word? Lead. That means exactly what it implies... you need to set the tone and the example. True leaders understand that to be a great leader is first to lead yourself.

132. You do not build a restaurant. You build a team, and your team builds your restaurant.

133. Sometimes the person who is holding your restaurant back from reaching its potential looks back at you in the mirror every morning.

134. You can't control your restaurant until you control your culture. That starts with you controlling yourself first.

135. Focus is your power. You can't control time. The only thing you can control is your focus and energy. Where focus goes, energy flows. Tap into that, and you'll see your productivity powers grow stronger than you could ever imagine.

136. Time is just a construct of the mind. You cannot change time or manipulate it. It is an uncontrollable variable that most people seem to be either chasing or a slave to. To break free from that, you need to look at your natural energy patterns, and when you are in the peak energy "zone" use that energy to get the right things done.

137. Your menu needs to be a representation of what you do best. Think of your menu like your greatest hits album. The Rolling Stones recorded 439 songs. When you go to a Stone's concert, do you want to hear those "B side" tracks or just the hits? Your menu needs to play your hits.

138. The goal of marketing is not to make a sale. It's to keep your brand top of mind. By achieving this level of brand recognition and top-of-mind awareness, restaurants are positioning their brand to be the first consideration when guest are ready to make a purchase. Over time, this can lead to increased guest loyalty, repeat business, and greater overall sales and success. #MoneyFollowsAttention

139. There is a vision of your restaurant that you have, and there is vision of your restaurant that your guests have. Somewhere in between is the restaurant it has to become.

140. Managers can be very hypocritical when it comes to "walking the talk." Leaders, on the other hand, say what they mean and do what they say. This key component alone will rocket you towards leadership because it builds trust with your team when you do exactly what you say. Integrity is not something that can be bought; it's a core value you live.

141. Managers "should" all over themselves all day long. Leaders take action and make it happen.

142. Leaders are always telling the team and their customers that they appreciate them and are grateful for what they bring to the business. When was the last time you told someone sincerely that you were grateful for them? Leaders know that when they put out positive energy, they get even more returned to them. Cultivate an attitude of gratitude and watch how your world changes.

143. Leaders never go backward. They only move forward. A true leader is someone who constantly strives to improve and find new solutions to problems, rather than looking to the past and dwelling on past failures or setbacks.

144. Maybe your sales have slumped because you lost touch with the fundamentals. The best way to recover from slow sales is to take a microscope to your existing operation - step-by-step - and make sure you're doing everything you can to ensure an outstanding guest experience.

145. The only thing holding your restaurant back is you. Talent and skill can take you to the top, but it's your character and mindset that keeps you there.

146. Lack of integrity is one of the main causes of brand dilution and team destruction.

147. Remember that the restaurant business is about people. It's about knowing your core values. It's how your words and actions work incongruence. Your restaurant is a living thing that you mold and shaped by the actions you take every day. Good or bad, your restaurant is a reflection of you!

148. Your restaurant will only progress when there is a true leader at its helm - someone who can admit their flaws and work to better them for the sake of their staff, customers, and business. With the right character, integrity, mindset, and momentum of a true restaurant leader, you'll defeat the real enemy within your restaurant and see enormous improvement.

149. Running a restaurant is relatively easy. It's the people puzzle that makes it complex, with all of the emotions and psychological biases that humans carry inside their brains, creating a fascinating puzzle. In short, it's people that make a restaurant work.

150. Too many restaurant owners operate with a noncommittal attitude. Your restaurant will never see the profits you want until you commit to doing whatever it takes to succeed. When failure is an option, there is a lack of commitment. Change is hard. The restaurant business can be a challenge. Get a mentor, a coach, or an advisor. Do something that puts you back in control of your restaurant.

151. Running a restaurant is a lot like playing chess. Each piece in the game has its strengths. Your job is to move each piece into a position where its natural strengths can become an asset.

152. Life is never really in balance. When you focus on an area, things tend to improve in that area. Focus on your relationship, and it tends to become better. Focus on marketing, and sales tend to increase. The real trick is to balance the time you focus on each area. That's the real balance.

153. If you do not control your time and focus, someone else will control it for you. You need to schedule as much as you can into your calendar. The gym, social media time, date nights, training with staff, lunch service, pre-shift, dinner service, marketing, R&D... everything. Use your calendar as the gatekeeper of your time.

154. Stop hiring for experience and instead focus more on personality. You can train skills (if they are trainable and coachable), you cannot change personality easily (even though most think they can).

155. If you truly want to have an impact on the people around you, then change yourself first. Be the example and set the standard. People are more likely to change when they see someone who inspires them. All improvement starts with self-improvement.

156. Watch the words and things you say because they form your reality.

157. Start small. Be steady. Commit. Stay the course. Adjust your habits to get the results you want. Become obsessed with becoming a better version of yourself.

158. Your restaurant will only reach the level of outstanding when you stop fighting amongst your team. Stop this bullshit of FOH vs BOH. Stop the internal competition between locations. A divided brand is a sign of weak leadership and a toxic culture.

159. Finding profits is not that hard if you're willing to swallow your pride a little and admit that you need to work at it. Make a commitment to nail down your numbers and know them like the back of your hand. Knowing your numbers will help you make better decisions every day, and that allows you to make adjustments that can add more to your bottom line.

160. Take control of your business by digging in and knowing your numbers. You can hire someone to do the work if you aren't good at this task, but you must be included and understand where every penny goes. Ignorance is not bliss, it's just ignorance.

161. Come to the reality that if you have people on your team who aren't lifting your brand, they're holding it down. You may have a sense of loyalty to them because they've been with you from the beginning, and you feel an obligation to take care of them—stop it. If they're not actively growing personally and professionally, they're dead weight, dragging down your business.

162. Get someone to hold you accountable. You need an outside person who isn't emotionally attached to you and who doesn't have an agenda to keep you on track. Accountability is the key element for those who reach their goals consistently.

163. What lies between desire and results is action. Saying you want a better restaurant and getting a better restaurant is the difference between mediocrity and success. There are a few things to get out in the open before you can make the jump to the next level.

164. If you're not growing both professionally and personally, you're dying a slow death of complacency. Better to go down fighting than to be forgotten due to lack of action.

165. Creating and growing a successful business is impossible without a solid foundation, also known as your vision. Though your strategy and operations will change as you gain perspective and insights, your business' vision will always remain the same.

166. Why do so many restaurants close? They didn't stand out. Being average (or even slightly above average) is a death sentence in an industry that's overwhelmingly oversaturated.

167. Human beings are fallible. We make mistakes. We mess things up. It's our mistakes that propel us forward to grow and evolve. It's in our DNA. Mistakes and learning go hand in hand. (If people make the same mistakes over and over that's a different problem altogether). People also want to be recognized for doing things right.

168. Marketing is not a one-time thing. It's a consistency thing. Throwing out that occasional video and then not really promoting it, is your downfall. You made a half-ass commitment, and the results show. If you want to play the social media marketing game, you need to put energy and effort in to get the results you want out.

169. In most working situations, it's the personalities of the team members and leaders that affect the day-to-day success of a restaurant.

170. Your words tell me what you say you want — your actions that tell me what you're willing to do to get it.

171. When I come to your restaurant, I'm not going to lower my standards so you're comfortable. I coach to make you and your business better; you can be mediocre all on your own.

172. Culture is the secret sauce that separates the good from the outstanding. Restaurants can have the same ingredients and even the same menu items. What separates them is the one thing that's hard to copy: culture.

173. Everything in the universe is energy. The energy you bring every day to your culture is either negative, neutral, or positive. Outstanding leaders are aware of their energy and how it feeds the culture they've built.

174. When you find weeds in your garden, you pull them, and spray weed killer to make sure more weeds don't grow in their place. When you find cultural weeds growing in your restaurant you must remove them, immediately.

175. Following the crowd is easy. The world is full of people who blindly follow the mainstream consciousness of thought and go along even when they know it's not right. Stop it. If you know it's not right, don't allow it.

176. A toxic culture is a symptom of a much deeper condition: the total absence of leadership.

177. If you think someone is lazy and entitled, you tend to find yourself surrounded by lazy and entitled people. Look and you will find. People are a complex puzzle of both good and bad traits. When you focus on the bad, you tend to get more of it.

178. If you have a Crab Culture, you need to isolate the crabs who are pulling down the team. It's time to step up and be the damn leader! You need to remove crab personalities from your organization, right now! It doesn't matter if they're an incredible sauté cook or are the server with the highest sales—destructive personalities only damage your culture and brand long term!

179. When you feel you don't deserve success, you're more likely to act out so that the mental scorecard in your subconscious is even. This is referred to as "protest behavior." You can only rise to the level of what you feel worthy of receiving.

180. If you only train your team to just do the job, you'll just get a temporary employee. If you invest in them to make them a better person, you'll develop a loyal team member.

181. When you have a solid culture that fosters learning, appreciation, and professionalism it will become a signal to the world that you're the employer of choice for restaurants in your market.

182. Old school managers who lead through fear are a dying breed, but they're still out there, clinging to outdated management techniques like "break them down and build them up." When people are broken down, they're rarely, if ever, built back up (in a positive, stronger way). Besides, do you really want broken people working in your restaurant and interacting with your hard-earned guests?

183. There is no room for an entitlement mindset on your team. None. It creates a passive team and there's no place in today's market for anyone on your team who's passive or uninterested about their work and their own development. The restaurant industry is changing and those who fail to adapt will become extinct.

184. An entitlement culture is often lazy with undercurrents of defiance and protest behavior, i.e., leaving early, not following through on tasks. This is a culture where the focus is on the individual rather than the guests you serve or the restaurant as a team.

185. Having an integrated training system is not about training people to do their job, it's about developing people so they can become better human beings, which in turn benefits them AND the restaurant.

186. Selection is critical to long-term restaurant success. Who you allow on your team is crucial to the development of an outstanding culture. Training is the fuel that feeds that culture.

187. Building a team is very much like creating a recipe; you must be very careful about the personalities that you put together. Too many strong or dominant members and you'll have a team loaded with people fighting over who's going to be in charge. The opposite can be just as debilitating; too many submissive members mean no one will step up to take the lead. It's definitely a balancing act.

188. Trust is the social glue that holds a team together. Without trust you don't really have a team; you have a collection of free agents all out for themselves. The Beatles told us that "all you need is love." For a team, what you really need is respect and trust.

189. There are two vital elements that contribute to an outstanding team member's success, skills & character (also known as core values). Skills get you into the game and character keeps you there.

190. Communication must flow unhindered from leadership to the team, among teammates, and from the team back to leadership. Too many restaurants communicate one way. When you communicate in only one direction, you're basically telling the team two things: you don't respect them, and you don't trust them.

191. Recruiting isn't placing help wanted ads on the Internet or social media — that's job advertising. No, you'll need to get out there and recruit.

192. Recruiting is a numbers game. It's a lot like digging for gold: You will have to sift through a lot of dirt to find a gold nugget.

193. 110 percent is BS! You can't give more than 100 percent, so please, for the love of all that is sacred, stop using this tired cliché! If most would (or could) just give 80 percent, they'd be astonished by their results. You only have 100 percent — aim for that and you're on the right track.

194. What you expect or focus on, you tend to get, much like a self-fulfilling prophecy. Focus on the perception that your staff is working against you, and you'll probably be "proven" right. It's funny how people rarely tend to exceed our expectations.

195. You are responsible for what you do. What actions you take. Personal accountability, at its core, is about taking action and doing exactly what you said you would do, when you said you would do it.

196. Hypocrisy runs rampant in the world, right alongside its cousin mediocrity. Those two travel together, running amok, laying siege to all the best intentions and plans.

197. Restaurants truly change when you stop talking, stop overthinking, and start doing.

198. You're the energy that creates the culture, good or bad. If leaders approach their restaurant with positivity, enthusiasm, and a focus on collaboration and growth, they can help to create a healthy and productive culture. On the other hand, negative attitudes, disruptive behaviors, and a lack of focus can contribute to a toxic culture that undermines the success of the restaurant. #OneBadAppleSpoilsTheBunch

199. We build better restaurants by building ourselves. Leaders are forged through chaos, pressure, and discipline. Anyone who says that leadership is easy is full of sh*t.

200. You'll never develop a high-performance team by standing in their way. You need to let them do their job, so they can learn and grow. You can't do their job for them, you have your own job to do..and that is being the leader.

201. Excellence, greatness, and market dominance require one critical element, and that's consistency.

202. When people don't respect themselves, it becomes rather apparent in their behavior. Your words say one thing, but your actions say everything. This behavior will manifest in many ways. One of the most common is overcompensating behavior. The person who is loud, obnoxious, and demeaning to others, is quite often suffering from a lack of confidence and self-respect for themselves. If people don't have respect for themselves, it's hard to get them to respect other things.

203. Never mistake being busy for being effective. You're rewarded for the results you get, not the effort.

204. Could you eat an entire cow? Yes, one steak at a time. I love this metaphor for approaching large or complex tasks. This mindset helps to make the task more manageable and less overwhelming, allowing leaders to focus on one step at a time and make progress towards the goal. Success comes when you have patience, persistence, and stay focused.

205. When you stop thinking in hours and commit to becoming more productive, you break free from the shackles of busywork and wasted effort.

206. Stop being held captive by a quest to find work/life balance and just live. Seek integration, not balance.

207. We've become addicted to busyness. Looking busy and declaring how busy we are is the new status symbol. When you say you're "so busy" what you're really saying is that you're too lazy to prioritize your day or life. You're stuck on the hamster wheel of life, running as fast as you can, getting nowhere.

208. Burnout isn't something that happens to you, it's something you do to yourself. it's important to note that burnout is not simply a response to stress, but rather the result of a combination of factors, including a person's coping mechanisms, lifestyle choices, and overall approach to stress. This means that burnout is not solely caused by external factors but can also be driven by one's own actions and decisions. In other words, burnout is not something that happens to you, but rather something you do to yourself through your attitudes and behaviors. By recognizing this, individuals have the power to take control and make positive changes to prevent and manage burnout.

209. You can't give to others without first giving to yourself. Self-care is not selfish, it's smart.

210. Working long hours in a restaurant is not a badge of honor, it's a mark of stupidity, piss poor planning, lack of priorities, failure to develop your team and schedule focus blocks, depletion of your internal energy levels, and fear of saying no. The answer isn't more hours, it's less bullsh*t. It's facing the truth.

211. Your menu is your number one marketing and profitability tool you have! Treat it with some respect.

212. Your ego is the brakes that hold you back from getting the results you truly want. The ego tells you that you know enough, so you stop learning. By focusing solely on maintaining the image that our ego has created, we limit our potential for growth and learning. This can cause us to miss opportunities for self-improvement and limit our ability to achieve our goals. On the other hand, when we are willing to let go of our ego and become open to new ideas and perspectives, we open ourselves up to new opportunities for growth and learning. This, in turn, can help us achieve our goals and reach new heights in both our personal and professional lives.

213. Contrary to the belief apparently held my many, people can't read minds. You must be the megaphone for who you are, what you do, and why you do it!

214. Here's the real secret to becoming a "sticky brand": It's not about you saying how great you are, it's about your guests saying how great you are!

215. Delusion is a powerful mental drug that keeps us stuck in average.

216. You can hold up the standards in your restaurant without being a jerk. You can be firm without insulting people. You can be a leader and not an asshole boss.

217. Does that mean train just until they get it right and say, "That's it, my job is done. They can do the task adequately."? No. Your duty as a leader is to train and train and train and train and train until they can't get it wrong.

218. Talk with your team, not down to your team.

219. Investing in your team's development will reduce your turnover.

220. If you don't know your numbers, you are part of the problem in your restaurant. Be the solution by getting a grip on your day-to-day numbers.

221. If you ask people to name someone, they thought was an outstanding leader and what about that person made them outstanding, here's what they would say: "They made me feel like I was important."

222. If you don't trust your team, you don't have a team. Instead, you have a bunch of mercenaries that job hop to the highest bidder.

223. Everyone gets stuck in a rut at some point in their life. The difference between winners and losers is that winners realize they're in a rut and take immediate action to get out. Losers stay down there, wallowing in the rut. They whine, kick, and complain until that shallow rut has now become their grave. You see, what separates the two is only the depth.

224. Great leaders stretch themselves first, then drive their team to become better. Failing to reach one's potential is the greatest waste in life.

225. When you look at the heart of the problems, drama, and chaos that seem to infect our industry, you find that poor communication is the underlying issue.

226. Great leaders always hold themselves to higher standards than they do for others. How you behave and act will become valuable examples for your team one way or another; you can be a leader to emulate or a fool to ignore. Your results depend on your actions, not just the words you say. Talk is truly cheap.

227. It's not very complicated to rise to the top of this industry because so many restaurants perform at an average level—it doesn't take much to pass them up. Staying on top, now that's a different story!

228. The basis of trust is giving it freely. People usually rise to our level of expectations. If you don't trust them, they tend to let you down. They'll also come to be distrustful of you. Trust lives in a realm of reciprocity—you only get it when you give it.

229. Leaders must always maintain focus and adjust the pace. True leaders kick up the team's energy to keep everyone on task and carry momentum through the slower times.

230. True leaders never say, "Well, my team should just know that." If they knew it, they would do it. Assumption is the root cause of communication issues.

231. The power to change your restaurant isn't held captive by tomorrow or next year, it's in the actions you take today. Like, right now today!

232. The results you experience in your restaurant or bar are in direct proportion to the quality of your communication skills. That is not an exaggeration, it's the truth. If you want a better brand, become obsessed with communicating to your team better. No bullshit, its life changing!

233. Get control of your emotions and your words before they cause havoc within your restaurant or bar. Avoid emotional reactions that cause you to lose credibility with your team Lose credibility, and its game over!

234. Leadership is about taking action and personal accountability. You can't sit on the sidelines, not playing in the game, hoping that you will somehow win. Leaders value action over words.

235. Leadership is never about having all the answers; it's about asking the right questions.

236. When you're around people in your personal and professional lives make sure you surround yourself with only those who elevate you. Avoid the negative energy vampires at all costs!

237. The past needs to be put exactly where it belongs... behind you. When you focus on it too much you lose the gift the current day offers.

238. Badass leaders articulate their visions, core values, and standards. They make it a daily ritual to talk to their teams. If you think that posting a memo on the wall telling the team your rules and policies is communicating...you are part of the problem.

239. Whatever the cause of the drama in your restaurant, here's a clue to stop it: drama needs an audience! If you don't participate and feed the fire that drama wants, it tends to fade away.

240. You want to be the restaurant in your market that out-trains your competition! Hey, other restaurants might be able to knock off your food and decor, don't let them out-train you! Refuse to lose the training game. Be the place that never stops getting better by always, always, always training.

241. If you can't find anything nice to say to your team, then why do you keep them around? Yes, they don't do everything right 100% of the time. Do you? It's easy to see the bad, try looking for the good for once.

242. To get more from life, you must become more. Sometimes that means growing and shedding things, habits, and sometimes friends that are trying to keep you suppressed and not growing. That's the old you and that version of you just gets you the same shit you have today. We all need growth. We all need challenge. We all need some goal out in front of us pulling us to it.

243. Words cannot move mountains, but they can move people to take action for a better life. Words can suppress or inspire you. Words can break people and they can build people. You have in your possession the most powerful tool to having a better relationship with your family, your team, your guests, and yourself...the words you use on a regular basis.

244. Stop being boring—care more about your social media posts!

245. If you always do what you've done, you'll remain exactly where you are now. Habits make the person; your social media habits make the marketing.

246. The secret to social media isn't much of a secret at all. It's about being social. It's about connecting with people. It's about sharing ideas. That means you're going to need to look past yourself and get involved in other people's interests. Share their posts. Like their pictures. Approach conversations as a two-way street. Oh, and please be sincere and authentic.

247. You must aim to become outstanding. You want your brand to stand out and set the pace for competition so every other restaurant in your market spends their time trying to catch you. It's always better to be the lead dog on a dogsled team.

248. It's time to ignore that little voice inside telling you this is all too much and instead tune into the voice that encourages you to own your market.

249. You become the best with consistency in both product and service.

250. Marketing is just a messenger for your brand. Sorry, but no amount of marketing will make up for a bad brand. Your brand is a combination of core values, purpose, and emotions. Those things are translated through the products you offer on your menu and the hospitality conveyed through your crafted guest experience.

251. The key is to remember that there are solutions to every problem. Sometimes, you just can't see the solution because you're stuck in a mindset that isn't serving you. To break free, you must change how you look at the problem and change your attitude about finding a solution.

252. Don't accept other people's opinions that "it can't be done" or "it won't work." Just because they haven't done it, doesn't mean you can't. People will try to get you to be "reasonable." The last thing you want to be is reasonable when you're going after the life you want.

253. A simple key to influencing your staff: just ask. That's all. Ask with clear directions, expectations, and reasons why. People who do things without having a "why" only comply out of fear. People who understand the why behind a request will commit to keeping the standards.

254. Stop thinking of your comfort zone as a place of comfort and see it for what it is: a place that causes you pain.

255. The greatest lies we tell are the ones we tell ourselves. It's true. You're a master at self-deception. You are adept at talking yourself into or out of anything! You have an entire league of misery living in your head telling you why you can't do the things that will improve you and your restaurant. Stop listing to them and start searching for the truth.

256. Think about this: What would it feel like to let go of all the bullshit, all the external pressures, every false expectation, and just be yourself? It's fucking freedom.

257. Your alter ego is your true self. You've done such a good job wearing the mask of who you think you need to be that you've likely forgotten who you really are.

258. The restaurant is your stage, and every night is a performance that allows you to participate in an event that elevates the human experience to a higher level. That's what restaurants truly do.

259. Fear is natural. It's a hard-wired human survival mechanism. Fear just needs to be acknowledged and respected, it doesn't need to be obeyed.

260. Knowing your purpose, vision, mission, or why you need to change is powerful. If you know the why, the how is easy. The biggest obstacle you may face is failing to connect with a powerful enough WHY that will drive you to change. Your purpose must be connected to strong emotions. You can think of lots of logical reasons why you should change but logic won't move you to act.

261. Without clear directions or standards, your team will create their own. *That usually is NOT good for you!*

262. The chokehold on any restaurant is the mindset of the owner and operators. You are your problems, and you are your solutions. You can get out of this by shifting your mindset.

263. Anything worth fighting for is worth the struggle and discomfort. The most successful restaurant operators are comfortable with being uncomfortable. Tony Robbins is the mind behind one of my favorite quotes, "The quality of your life is in direct proportion to the amount of uncertainty you can comfortably deal with."

264. Energy creates atmosphere and is the hidden "it" factor that creates a great guest experience and then transforms it into exceptional! Here's the secret: people are energy. You're in control of the energy you bring into your restaurant.

265. Managers come to work and just do enough of their jobs to get by. Leaders learn to become better people.

266. Most of your attention should be focused on leveraging your strengths, because those are what sets you apart and speaks to your guests. That is how you become outstanding!

267. Thinking outside the box can be a dangerous trap. Problems arise when we want to innovate just for the sake of innovation. Many people want to do the new thing, few want to do the right thing. If you want to be the best at what you do, make sure everything is in order inside the box before you venture outside it.

268. Reaction is how most respond to situations. It's primal and emotional. It also is volatile hard to control. When you react, you show people you don't have control and that erodes trust among your team.

269. The most successful restauranteurs adopt a mindset to be proactive. Reactionary mindset looks to solve the problem now. Proactive mindsets look to prevent problems before they start. They look ahead to see potential issues. Reactive managers are playing checkers. Proactive leaders are thinking far ahead like in a chess game.

270. If there's one superpower you need, it's consistency! Habits only change through constant repetition and reinforcement. You can't do something once or twice and think that's it. Nope—you have to work at it until it becomes unconscious, automatic. If you need to think about it, it's not wired deeply enough to your neural network (your brain) to become second nature. True success comes when your bad habits are replaced with positive habits. They make or break restaurants and people.

271. You can have the best systems in the world, but if you don't have a plan to strategically use those systems, you're going to fail because you have no direction.

272. The funny thing about change is that it doesn't want to materialize. We tend to want 296 others to change so we can stay the same. Has anyone ever suggested that you change and explained that they're fine just the way they are? I'm sure you have. Hypocrisy runs rampant in the world. Don't succumb to it. Rise above it and be willing to fight for what you want in life.

273. To really change and reach your goals you need to not only have the right priorities, but you also have to put them in the correct order. Success is like a combination lock: if you don't enter the digits (priorities) in the right order you'll never open it (reach your potential).

274. The only thing you have control of is this moment. Taking action now is the cure for procrastination! You just need to get your ass moving in the right direction and let momentum help you achieve your goals. Success breeds more success, and once your high-achieving, badass self gets a taste of it, you'll want even more.

275. One common issue many restaurants face...**you can't see the problem if you are the problem.**

276. **Ego, pride, denial, and mediocrity** are the top four reasons restaurants really close.

277. Hope is great for somethings, it's a horrible strategy for running a restaurant.

278. Sometimes the things that choke out the growth of a restaurant is the owner in the wrong position in their company.

279. Here's the cold hard truth: if you are not happy will your life the way it is, then do something about it! Just stop whining and crying about it.

280. If you don't know your numbers, you don't know your business. You have more of a hobby than a business...a very expensive hobby.

281. One of the main reasons for turnover is unclear standards and unspoken expectations.

282. Restaurant success is not rocket science...*it's people science.*

283. The problem with that is when you seek outside validation, it might not ever come. Then what? You're stuck on a never-ending treadmill of seeking approval. When I understood that the only approval, I needed was from myself, it changed my life.

284. Stop looking outward for solutions and start looking inward. You can change your menu. You can change the decor. You can change your staff. You can even change locations. However, if you don't change you, your mindset as the leader none of it matters. Your restaurant reflects you as a leader. Your habits. Your passion. Your beliefs.

285. 20% of restaurant success is systems and strategy. The 80% is the mental game it's mindset. You must know you. What are you good at, what are you marginal at, and what do you suck at.

286. Labor is problematic everywhere in the world. You need to invest and spend time developing your culture to attract better people. Culture flows down not up and that starts with you. Culture is a magnet and attracts people to your business. Start showing the human side of your brand on social media. Those food and beverage pictures are nice; however, they don't show me who you are and what you're really about besides pretty food and drink. Tell me a story and take me on a journey. All people, whether it's your guests or potential staff, want to be taken on a journey. Become a tour guide to take them on that journey.

287. Obsession gets a bad reputation. Sure, an obsession can be bad if it controls you. However, if you control it that can evaluate you past ordinary to extraordinary. I understood early that all business problems are really people problems in disguise. Solve the people problems and the business problems start to disappear.

288. Your habits predict your level of performance. Habits are routine behaviors that are repeated regularly and tend to occur subconsciously. They play a critical role in shaping one's performance, as they can either positively or negatively impact an individual's level of success. Habits that are aligned with one's goals and values have a positive effect on performance, while those that undermine these goals can have a negative effect. Your habits are strong indicators of your level of success, and conscious effort to develop and maintain positive habits can lead to improved performance in your restaurant.

289. When you're a commodity, and you compete, your market judges you on price. It's hard to build loyalty because when people are addicted to the price, they jump ship as soon as another restaurant down the street as a better price. Now when you dominate, you become the brand of choice. People always drive past average to get to exceptional.

290. That culture is comprised of a few things. One being core values and I cannot emphasize enough how powerful core values are. They are what separates the average from the outstanding — not just having cool words for a poster. Everyone has those feel-good words on their core value list, yet few live them. If you can't strive to be an example of the core values your brand has, then they are not a core value, it's just wishful thinking.

291. I've talked about this before that people buy emotions over logic. Yeah, that vegetarian entree is good for your body, that's logical. If you offer it because you had three close friends who died young from heart issues, and you want to provide healthy options for our guests. That's emotion. That's heart. That's character. People don't buy what you do; they buy why you do it.

292. Remember that trust is everything when it comes to building brand loyalty. In the long run, a strong reputation built on trust can lead to sustainable success and make a brand stand out in a competitive marketplace.

293. Everyone has a story behind the restaurant. It doesn't matter if you're a family-owned business now run by the great-grandchildren, a lawyer decided he hated practicing law want to follow his dream to be a chef or the mom who wanted to start a gluten-free line of entrées for home meal replacements. We all have a story to tell. ***The sad thing is that most restaurants and bars do not tell their story.*** Instead, they promote their food and beverage.

294. If you truly want to get control of your life it all starts here by taking control of your mindset! Stop the blame game and step up to the reality that you are in charge of how you respond to life events. Notice that last sentence mentioned the word "respond". Here is where the power of words comes into play. If you go to the doctor and they say you are having a "reaction" to the medication...that's bad. If they say you are "responding" to the medication...that's great! Each day when things happen you have a choice to either react or respond.

295. One key is to know is the difference between compliance and commitment. Compliance is the default mode of the average worker. They do just enough work to keep their job. They do things based on your reasons. Their heart isn't into their job and most just go through the motions. No heart. No passion. Just working for that paycheck. When you can get your team to find a reason that resonates with their values and it personal, then you get commitment. Now they do things based on their reasons and not just yours. This leads us to see that true motivation is an inside job. Looking back at our compliance versus commitment discussion...what those two really are in psychology speak is extrinsic motivation (compliance) and intrinsic motivation (commitment).

296. Your restaurant and your life will never (I mean never ever) improve until you step up and take total accountability for everything that happens in your restaurant and your personal life!

297. The secret to getting your business back under control so you can have more time for what matters is culture. Culture is the cure.

298. Client: My business in just in a rut. Me: The only difference between a rut and a grave is the depth.

299. Your biggest motivation should be the fear of being average!

300. If you would turn all those things, you know you should do into a must do, you would have a totally different restaurant.

301. The key to not having your restaurant run you? Build your restaurant around your life, not your life around your restaurant!

302. The relationship you have with yourself is the relationship you have with your restaurant.

303. Your restaurant is a reflection of your habits. Period.

304. My job as your coach isn't to give you a pass on your bullshit. My job is to get you to deal with your bullshit!

305. The best advice I ever received was only five words....You'll want to quit, don't.

306. You can't control your restaurant if you can't control yourself.

307. The only thing standing between you and the restaurant you know it can be is the bullshit excuse you keep telling yourself as to why you can't get it.

308. If you would turn all those things, you know you should do into a must do, you would have a totally different restaurant.

309. Every challenge you face is an opportunity to change some of your old habits, drop the excuses (bullsh*t), and transform yourself into the badass you were meant to be.

310. Leadership is always the problem; leadership is also always the solution.

311. Conversation with a line cook...Line Cook: What's your problem with me? Me: you don't respect yourself, which is your problem. You don't respect the food, that's my problem.

312. Don't tell me you have to do everything yourself because you don't trust your team. That is bullshit! If you do not trust your people to do their jobs, then find people you do! A true leader does not stand in the way of their team. I have a saying that if you cannot spot the negative person in your restaurant bringing everyone down...it's you.

313. The biggest mistake a restaurant can make it not to think of itself as a business.

314. If you really want success, then you must back yourself into a corner. Give yourself no choice but to succeed. Let the consequences of failure become so horrific and so unthinkable that you'll have no choice but to do whatever it takes to get the restaurant and life you really want!

315. Restaurants get destroyed the most from the inside.

316. Failure is never fatal. But failing to change might be.

317. If your restaurant is not 100% the way you want it, then you have to admit that it just might suck a little.

318. Your greatest danger is your ego and how it makes you unconsciously maintain illusions about yourself. These may be comforting in the moment, but in the long run they make you defensive and unable to learn or progress. When you stop learning or progressing, you start dying. Maybe not quickly, just a little more each day.

319. Saying you are too busy is really saying to me that you're too lazy to prioritize your life.

320. Normal ideas and normal actions lead to a normal life. Fuck normal! You don't get all you want out of life by being normal! Aim for outstanding and get it ALL...anything less is a waste of your untapped potential.

321. It doesn't matter what is true only what you believe is true because with work that will become true. Your thoughts create your beliefs, your beliefs become your reality. The universal theory of everything and the master algorithm of evolution is: Beliefs > Actions > Results > Feedback. You must intercept your own algorithm at the beliefs stage, take massive action with your new beliefs, experience your results, listen to feedback, and then iterate your beliefs and actions again and again each time to perfect the process.

322. Where you are in life, your current situation, it's all your doing. You built yourself and your life and it's you who's solely responsible for where you are right now and where you got in the future. There is no external force, person or thing against you -it's all you.

323. We are not the highest version of ourselves which we can imagine. We are the lowest version of ourselves which we tolerate. Understand that you will never achieve your dreams if you don't fight like hell to not compromise your standards. If you want to achieve your dreams and goals, you must turn your standards into nonnegotiable standards.

324. The key to all evolution is variation and when you start to grow tired of what is in the light you must face what is in the dark. We must understand the dualism that exists in our mind and loose the binary stance of one true right and wrong and one true me and not me. Nothing is static and everything in this universe is forever becoming. The real question is: "Who am I becoming?"

325. Our minds are an on/off system that are programmed over time to believe certain things and our experience of reality is simply the result of those beliefs. When we experience something or think of something we stack a rock on a particular set of scales, either positive or negative. Each belief is a scale and whatever side has the most rocks on it that's what we believe. What we believe is our reality. Remember that perception is projection.

326. Be constantly aware of mental feedback loops. What one thinks is what one thinks about. A circular relationship where cause creates effect and effect bends back around and feeds back into cause in a self-fulfilling prophesy. Mental feedback loops can build you up to be the best in the world or break you down till you consider quitting. Make sure you catch the downs and feed the ups. Always manage your emotional state.

327. Most people's character has become so strong and defined that it's reversed the roles and pulling the strings on its own master. You have to pin your character down and define exactly who it is and what it's capable of and then figure out what you really want to achieve in life and see if that character is fit for the job If the character isn't fit for the job, it's time to design one who will achieve it with ease and make the conscious decision to grow into it. Your character is changeable, and **you** pull the strings.

328. Don't just get things done. Do the work that matters. Reflect on the person you want to be this week. How can you align your actions with your intentions?

329. Who makes you smarter? While it feels great to accomplish something on your own, some of the best work we do is with the help of others. Who can help you make your work even better?

330. Small steps add up to big results. Sometimes the best way to tackle a big task is to break it down into smaller steps. Brainstorm how you can break down a current or upcoming task into smaller, more achievable steps. The only way to eat an entire cow is one steak at a time!

331. Focus on the positive. It is so easy to notice what is going wrong. But what is going right? Make a list of things that are going well right now and appreciate your part in making them happen.

332. Let shit go. Are you holding onto things that no longer serve you? This could be anything from negative friends to personal grudges, all of which take up unproductive space in your life. What can you let go of today?

333. Today be a better listener. The greatest gift you can give to people is your time and attention. What questions can you ask so that you learn something new about someone on your team?

334. Actions speak louder than words. Success isn't loud. Success speaks for itself. What is something you have been intending to do, but haven't done yet? What is one action you can complete today to turn that idea into reality?

335. Streamline your workflow. When you're good at what you do, a lot depends on you. But that can slow the process down. Where can you delegate responsibility, so that work can flow around you?

336. #WTSD: Problems are opportunities! Reframe the way you see a problem. What if you took it as an opportunity to learn? Look for the positives to be gained by overcoming a problem.

337. Remember that "slow is smooth and smooth is fast". The fastest approach isn't always the best approach. It's okay to slow down. It gives you a chance to notice things and make smarter decisions. What areas of your life would benefit from a slower and more attentive approach?

338. The next time you're faced with a tough decision, try comparing options based on as many factors as you can: time, money, core values, sacrifices, etc. The more thorough your review, the more confident you can be in your final call.

339. You must set a daily intention. Your mindset has more control over your day than you might think. Set an intention for your day — it can be something you want to do, a way you want to feel, or anything that inspires you. Giving your day a direction can help you see things in a new way and get more meaning out of your actions.

340. If you truly want massive success here is the secret: Make the people around, you better! When the people around you succeed, it lifts everyone up. How can you be encouraging to the people around you this week?

341. Leaders are reader! Block off time today to learn. The smartest people are always learning. What is a lesson you can take away from a recent experience?

342. Take control of your emotional states by acting the way you want to feel! No one has more control over how you feel than you do. If you don't like how, you've been feeling lately, what can you do to change that?

343. Peak Performance Secret - Plan your perfect day. What would it look like if today went perfectly? How can you help things fall into place? Where do you have areas for flexibility? With a clear vision, you are more likely to achieve the results you want.

344. Leader boosts their credibility by being a positive example. Show don't tell. What are some actions you can take this week that will help you earn the respect of those around you? What can you do to be the leader?

345. The secret to getting shit done is focus! Focus always takes you further. Instead of trying to accomplish everything, try giving all of your energy to one or two really important projects or goals today.

346. You can do anything, but not everything. There are only so many hours in the day. What are your top priorities? What deserves your focus, and what can you let go of?

347. Leaders grow their gratitude daily. Who are you grateful for? What little things make your days special? Write a list of the people, places, and things that you are thankful to have in your life.

348. The most successful are persistent and consistent. If you want to be successful, the best thing you can do is practice consistency. How are you doing on your monthly challenges? Where do you fall short in implementing good habits? Be honest with yourself. If you don't like the answers you just gave, then change your actions!

349. Schedule time for self-care. Do something today that makes you feel good. Treat it like any other appointment and schedule it on your calendar. It could be as big as a spa day or as small as a quiet cup of coffee to yourself.

350. Remember to manage your minutes! Where are you losing time throughout the day? What tasks are you still doing that you could delegate or stop altogether?

351. If you feel stuck remember that old ways won't open new doors. If you do what you've always done, you'll keep getting the same results. What are some new ways to solve a recurring problem in your life? Brainstorm and see if inspiration strike — it might just be the start of something big.

352. Today celebrate your wins. There is always more work to do, so if you don't set aside time to acknowledge and celebrate your wins, they will just pass you by. What is a recent success? Who can you share it with? Why is it meaningful?

353. Trust your gut. When it comes to decision-making, we usually rely on logic. But what does your gut tell you? What might your intuition be telling you about a certain situation?

354. Design your life backwards. Imagine where you want to be in 10 years. Your MAP (Massive Action Plan) needs to show your destination. Now think about where you are now. What is one thing you can do today to move in the direction of the life you want to live?

355. Time to reflect on your journey...You have come a long way this year. How have you changed since you first started this year? How will your experiences this year inform your goals and actions next year?

356. You have complete control over only one thing in the universe — your thinking!

357. You learn more from failure than from success. Don't let it stop you. Failure. Builds. Character.

358. Creating new habits and rewiring your brain is not easy. If it were, everyone would be living their life to their potential without any backsliding. Real life is not like that! It takes constant and steady pressure to change yourself. That is why the concept of Kaizen is SO IMPORTANT to our new way of looking at ourselves and our restaurants. Every day you make minor improvements.

359. If your restaurant runs smoothly and the profits are great, you have more good habits than bad habits. Now, if running your restaurant is more like a cage-death match and profits seemed like a roller coaster ride, then you have more bad habits than good habits. Here is some good news: habits are learned behaviors.

360. Hiring is the gatekeeper that protects that culture. When you take short cuts and don't conduct and solid interview you let in those that might damage your culture. It only takes one bad apple to ruin culture.

361. When you commit to a course of action and a new plan you want to be monomaniacal in your focus. This is the path you want, and you will reach your destination! Is it always smooth sailing? Hell no! Hey, boats are safest in the harbor, but that's not what boats are built for! You got to get out into the sea!

362. There's a saying of Elite Special Operation Teams: *"If it walks like a duck and talks like a duck, better have a plan in case it's a chicken."*

363. Leaders set standards high and do the right things to move the company forward. They get up on their soapbox and talk daily about company core values, building the brand, and strengthening the team. Many restaurants cling to outdated management theories that don't resonate with today's workers. Management is dead—leadership is where it's at.

364. *To have a profitable restaurant requires just one thing...discipline.* #WriteThisShitDown: Discipline = Freedom. Now, fair warning...it is a very simple equation that will challenge you every second of everyday to implement. When your why is bigger than your how, you'll make it happen.

365. Remember this, one day you will die. Time doesn't care what you do with it so do something worthy of who you are... The phrase "Aude aliquid dignum" is Latin for "dare something worthy" which emphasizes the idea that we should strive to do things that are worthy of who we are and leave a lasting impact. The reminder that one day we will die is meant to bring a sense of urgency and encourage us to prioritize what truly matters and make the most of our time on earth. This is a reminder to live a life filled with purpose and meaning, rather than just existing and letting time pass by. By doing things that align with our values and passions, we can ensure that our time on earth was well-spent and we leave a legacy that we can be proud of. Less talk and more action.

Take the daily inspirations listed here and do something with them. Words on paper are just potential. You must bring them to life by your actions.

Thousands of restaurants have been through my coaching programs and each of them found that taking massive action got them over the hump of those days when you just don't feel like it.

Fuck your feelings!

Do the work and you will see results. *That I guarantee.*

READY TO GET THE RESTAURANT YOU WANT?

It starts by joining my #1 Group Coaching Program for Independent Restaurants called **The Restaurant Coach™ University.**

For just $97 a month you get **2 Hours of LIVE Coaching** with me personally + access to my **private training library** + an invite to my **secret community** where you can ask questions and get answers 7-days a week from myself and members.

WANT MORE?

School is never out for the true professional. If you have applied the principles outlined in the booklet, you will see some fantastic results. The beautiful thing about getting a taste of success is you want more!

Grab a copy of my booklet called Outstanding Mindset. It will give you a step-by-step guide to having an Outstanding Day! This booklet is available on Amazon exclusively. Plus, I included several bonuses along with this informative booklet!

You will have to do the work and apply the principles in this book to get results. Many will get this book, read it, and not do one thing new to get the life they want. I am betting you are not like that. You will take action, and you will get results. Just make sure to create new habits and to keep on yourself. Change is never easy. If it were, everyone would have the life and restaurant they want...***we know that most don't.***

THE RESTAURANT COACH™ PODCAST

is another *free* resource that you just need to subscribe to so you never miss an episode. Interviews with leading restaurant experts, tools, and tips to get you the restaurant and life you want.

THE RESTAURANT COACH™ (TRC) *NATION*

> *"A lot of people put pressure on themselves and think it will be way too hard for them to live out their dreams. Mentors are there to say, 'Look, it's not that tough. It's not as hard as you think. Here are some guidelines and things I have gone through to get to where I am in my career.'"*
>
> — Joe Jonas

I started **TRC Nation** as a place where sisters and brothers from the restaurant industry could gather to get solutions to real issues they face every day. Not a place to bitch and complain about how much the industry sucks, but a place where positive attitudes prevail. I truly love this industry with all my heart, and if you become a member of TRC Nation, you do too, even if you might have fallen out of love with it.

The spirit of hospitality is what drives us, and I wanted to help bring that back to the restaurant world. To do that I wanted to **start** a **mentoring** program for restaurant leaders (at all levels) **to start** the revolution to bring back the core values that the restaurant world once had: respect, integrity, compassion, humility, and service to others.

TRC Nation is honored to have a growing list of world-class industry experts (mentors) that are willing to donate some time each week (for an 8-week program) to help others rekindle that spark and find direction in a turbulent industry.

Each mentor has been hand-picked by myself for the experience they offer and the value they bring every day to raise the standards in the restaurant industry.

How do you get a mentor? It's easy. First, apply to join **TRC Nation on Facebook** and then apply to get a mentor from the post talking about the program! Just hit **'Sign Up'** and the road to getting everything you want begins! See you inside TRC Nation!

GET AN ACCOUNTABILITY PARTNER. THAT MEANS A COACH!

Do you have a coach?

If not, you could be limiting your restaurant's success. That's because coaches help you identify and focus on what's important, which accelerates your success. Great coaches:

- Create a safe environment in which people see themselves more clearly.
- **Identify gaps between where the client is and where the client needs or wants to be**

- **Ask for more intentional thought, action and behavior changes than the client would have asked of him or herself**
- **Guide the building of the structure, accountability, and support necessary to ensure sustained commitment**

Successful athletes understand the power of coaching. The United Kingdom Coaching Strategy describes the role of the sports coach as one that "*enables the athlete to achieve levels of performance to the degree that may not have been possible if left to his/her endeavors.*"

Innovative restaurant brands understand that coaching can help their leadership team increase their performance at work. They invest in coaching for their senior leaders and high potential employees

Coaching also has an impact on an organization's financial performance; according to an International Coaching Federation study, 60% of respondents from organizations with strong coaching cultures report their revenue to be above average, compared to their peer group. Coaching pays for itself when applied.

If you are starting a restaurant and want to set yourself up for success right from the start or if you are an existing restaurant that wants more... coaching is the ultimate tool.

Now is coaching for everyone, of course not. That's why I am willing to give you're a FREE one-hour introductory coaching session so you can see if coaching is right for you and your restaurant.

Follow the link to get started with a FREE Coaching Session

www.therestaurantcoach.com

*Restaurant coaching is not for everyone. Side effects include increased profits, better staff happier guests, stronger brand identity, reduced stress, improved relationships, and quality sleep Talk to The Restaurant Coach™ to see if coaching is right for you.

ABOUT DB

Donald Burns is The Restaurant Coach™, named one of **The Top 50 Restaurant Experts to Follow and one of 23 Inspiring Hospitality Experts to Follow on Twitter**. He is the leading authority, speaker, and international coach on how restaurant owners, operators, and culinary professionals go from just **good** to becoming **outstanding.**

A former USAF Pararescueman (PJ), restaurant owner, and Executive Chef with Wolfgang Puck has the unique skills to break restaurants free from average and skyrocket them to peak performance. He works with restaurants that want to **build their brand**, **strengthen their team**, and **increase their profits** without sacrificing their lives to their business.

He is the author of:

Your Restaurant Sucks! *Embrace the suck. Unleash your restaurar Become outstanding.*

Your Restaurant STILL Sucks! *Stop playing small. Get what you war Become a badass.*

Your Restaurant Culture Sucks! Stop surviving. Start thriving. Escape mediocrity.

Pick up your copy at Amazon! **Available in Kindle, Hard Cover and Paperback Formats.**

All books are also available in audiobook format over at Audible.com

www.ingramcontent.com/pod-product-compliance
Lightning Source LLC
Chambersburg PA
CBHW070242220526
45465CB00004B/1487